Our Global Village

Germany

By: PJ Lents
Illustrated by: Larry Nolte

Milliken Publishing Company   St. Louis, Missouri

My special thanks to Ruthild Kronberg for sharing her knowledge of games played by children in Germany, and to my husband, John, for his support.

To my parents, Calvin and Edith Carpenter—PJL

Milliken Publishing Company
1100 Research Blvd.
St. Louis, MO 63132

Editor: Cindy Follman
Managing Editor: Kathy Hilmes

ISBN 1-55863-267-0

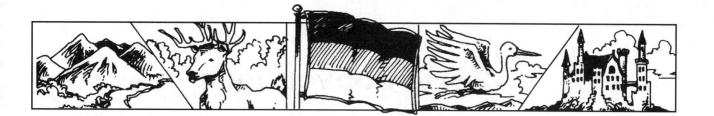

A Multicultural Experience

Our Global Village hopes to share ideas, hands-on activities, and resources from other cultures which will lead you, your students, and their families in different experiences. Learning how others live, think, and react is becoming increasingly important. The earth is a global village, and each of us is quickly affected by events, styles, disasters, and ideas from far away. Old barriers of mountains and oceans are disappearing with fax machines and airplanes. It is important to help young children learn about and value the diversity in the world around them. Fortunate is the child who has the opportunity to interact with people who speak different languages, who eat different foods, and whose skins are different colors. This child will come to appreciate the fascinating differences between people in the world while learning that people are much the same. We hope this resource series will help to create a multicultural community in your classroom as you learn and share different languages, customs, and celebrations.

Metric Conversions

The purpose of this page is to aid in the conversion of measurements in this book from the English system to the metric system. Note that the tables below show two types of ounces. Liquid ounces measure the volume of a liquid and have therefore been converted into milliliters. Dry ounces, a measure of weight, have been converted into grams. Because dry substances, such as sugar and flour, may have different densities, it is advisable to measure them according to their weights in ounces rather than their volumes. The measurement unit of the cup has been reserved solely for liquid, or volume, conversions.

Conversion Formulas					
when you know	formula	to find			
		when you know	formula	to find
teaspoons	x 5	milliliters	x .20	teaspoons
tablespoons	x 15	milliliters	x .60	tablespoons
fluid ounces	x 29.57	milliliters	x .03	fluid ounces
liquid cups	x 240	milliliters	x .004	liquid cups
US gallons	x 3.78	liters	x .26	US gallons
dry ounces	x 28.35	grams	x .35	dry ounces
inches	x 2.54	centimeters	x .39	inches
square inches	x 6.45	sq. centimeters	x .15	square inches
feet	x .30	meters	x 3.28	feet
square feet	x .09	square meters	x 10.76	square feet
yards	x .91	meters	x 1.09	yards
miles	x 1.61	kilometers	x .62	miles
square miles	x 2.59	sq. kilometers	x .40	square miles
Fahrenheit	$(°F-32)x5/9$	Celsius	$(°Cx9/5)+32$	Fahrenheit

Equivalent Temperatures
32°F = 0°C (water freezes)
212°F = 100°C (water boils)
350°F = 177°C
375°F = 191°C
400°F = 204°C
425°F = 218°C
450°F = 232°C

Common Cooking Conversions
1/2 cup = 120 milliliters
12 fluid ounces = 354.88 milliliters
1 quart (32 oz.) = 950 milliliters
1/2 gallon = 1.89 liters
1 Canadian gallon = 4.55 liters
8 dry ounces, 1/2 pound = 227 grams
16 dry ounces, 1 pound = 454 grams

Table of Contents

Germany 1

History 4

Language Expression 7

Daily Life 9

Foods 12

Games 15

Arts and Sciences 17

Holidays 21

Additional Resources 24

GERMANY

Hamburg

Elbe River

Oder River

Berlin ☆

Leipzig ●

Dresden ●

Rhine River

Bonn ●

Frankfurt ●

Black Forest

Danube River

Munich ●

Bavarian Alps

Germany

After World War II, Germany was divided into two countries—West Germany and East Germany. The city of Berlin, the former capital, was divided by a wall emphasizing the separateness of these two nations. Many neighborhoods and families were split apart when the wall was built. East Germany was a political satellite of the Soviet Union and West Germany was an ally of the United States. On October 3, 1990, East and West Germany were formally reunited. The reunification of Germany has been the cause of much rejoicing for the German people. It will also call for many changes as two very different countries again become one.

Name—Bundesrepublik Deutschland

Population—77,536,000

Size—137,778 square miles (358,222 square kilometers)

Climate—temperate

Major cities—Most people live in the cities.
    Bonn—the capital of West Germany when East and West Germany were divided*
    Berlin—the capital of Germany*
    Frankfurt—the commercial center
    Hamburg—the country's largest seaport
    Munich—the capital of Bavaria
    Leipzig—the host of the well-known Leipzig Book Fair
    Dresden—a cultural center for hundreds of years

Language—The national language is German. High German is the most commonly spoken form of German, though a number of other German dialects are spoken in different parts of the country.

Flag—The German flag has three equally sized horizontal stripes. The uppermost stripe is black, the middle stripe is red, and the bottom one is gold.

At this printing, much of the government is still run from the former West German capital of Bonn as many of the government offices are still there.

In Your Classroom

Make a German flag. Use construction paper or paints. Use the flag on a bulletin board as a centerpiece for a display of pictures and information about Germany.

Trace or copy a map of Germany. Remember to trace all of Germany, not just the East or the West. Show children the borders where Germany was divided. Be sure they realize Berlin was also divided into East and West Germany.

Physical Features

There are several different landscapes in Germany. The Northern Lowlands are sandy plains that were formed by glaciers. The Central Uplands have large rock masses and mountain ranges that are old and worn down by erosion. These mountain ranges which include the Ore, the Harz, the Thuringer Wald, the Taunus, and the Rhineland Slate are heavily wooded. Trees found in this area include pine, beech, spruce, and oak. The southern hill country and the Black Forest are popular with tourists. Some people say the Black Forest was given its name because of the dark green color of its pine trees; others think it earned its name due to the density of the trees that allowed very little light into the forest. The Bavarian Alps consist of only a few of the mountains that form the Alps. One of the highest peaks in the range is in Germany. It is the Zugspitze which is 9,721 feet (2,916 meters) high.

The climate in Germany is moderate even though the country is so far north. One reason for the mild temperatures is the North Atlantic Drift, an ocean current which warms western winds in the winter and cools them in the summer. The temperatures vary according to region. Winter temperatures vary from 21° to 34° F (-6° to 1° C), and summer temperatures range from 61° to 70° F (16° to 21° C). It rains frequently in Germany.

Germany has many rivers. The Danube, the Rhine, the Elbe, and the Oder are four of the main rivers. Rivers are used for recreation as well as transportation and industry.

The area around the Rhine provides the best farmland in Germany. Farmers in this area primarily grow grapes for wine, berries, and fruit trees. Wheat, rye, potatoes, and sugar beets are grown in other areas of Germany.

Native animals in Germany include deer, wild boar, bears, wolves, foxes, otters, badgers, wildcats, sea eagles, and white storks. Most of these animals can only be found deep in the forest. White storks may be seen nesting on chimneys of houses in more rural areas. Herring, mackerel, and cod are found in coastal waters.

Because Germany is an industrialized nation, pollution is a concern for many people. Although laws now prevent the dumping of chemicals into rivers, numerous rivers have already become polluted causing many fish to die. Many of the trees in Germany, especially in the famous Black Forest, are diseased or dead due to acid rain and other pollutants. These concerns have led to the organization of a new political party called the Green Alternative.

Some areas of what was formerly East Germany were heavily industrialized and had no controls on pollution in effect. These areas are now severely damaged. It will be extremely expensive to repair the damage in these areas, if the damage can be repaired at all.

In Your Classroom

Discuss the different types of pollution and the effects pollution has on nature. What are some ways to control pollution? How can each child contribute to help keep the environment clean?

Castles

During the Middle Ages, many kingdoms in Germany were weak, and fighting was a frequent occurrence as various people tried to gain power and land. Castles were built for protection. Many castles were built throughout Europe between 1050 and 1350.

The earliest castles were built of wood. Each one had a tower and outbuildings that were protected by a strong wooden fence. In the eleventh century, stone was used in place of wood. Stone would not burn and was harder to break through than wood. Stone walls were built to replace wooden fences. In time, castles became larger. Their towers were rounded, and an extra wall was added to help defend the tower.

Castles were built in places that would be easy to defend. Many were built on steep hillsides or on top of rocky cliffs. In areas that were flat, great mounds were made of rocks and earth, and the castles were built on these.

One of the castles built on the banks of the Rhine was the Marksburg Castle—the only castle to escape capture during the Thirty Years War. It still stands today in Braubach, Germany.

In Your Classroom

Make a model of a castle. Include a gatehouse, drawbridge, towers, and a moat. See the Additional Resources section for books with directions.

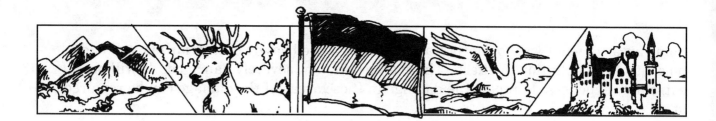

History

Germany was inhabited by several different tribes for many years. They were controlled by the Roman empire for a time. The tribes eventually overthrew the Romans and created hundreds of constantly changing, small kingdoms.

Karl der Grosse, or Charlemagne, incorporated Germany as a part of his empire. In 800 A.D., he was crowned emperor by the Pope. He encouraged people in his empire to learn to read and write, sponsored artists and musicians, and formed a central government and court system. All of this lasted until his death, at which time his empire was divided into three kingdoms.

Most of the area that is present day Germany was ruled by Louis the German, one of Charlemagne's grandsons. He was not as strong a leader as his grandfather had been, and eventually local dukes and counts grew to have more power than the kings in Germany.

In 1517, Martin Luther, a Catholic priest, protested many of the practices of the Catholic Church. This began the Protestant Reformation which led to many wars. The worst of these wars was the Thirty Years War which lasted from 1618 to 1648 and involved some of Germany's neighboring countries. The Treaty of Westphalia ended the Thirty Years War. It created a Germany that was a series of small states and city-states which each had its own system of government and religion.

Prussia became the strongest of the states. It was ruled by Frederick the Great from 1740 to 1786. Frederick created laws against torture and religious discrimination and encouraged freedom of the press.

In the early 1800s, Germans fought Napoleon and his French armies as he tried to expand France's territory. Many areas of Germany were ruled by the French for a time. After Napoleon was defeated, the Congress of Vienna met and created thirty-nine German states.

In 1871, Otto von Bismarck, the chancellor of Prussia, united Germany. King Wilhelm I was crowned kaiser, or emperor, of Germany, and all the states were united into one kingdom. This made Prussia the center of political and economic power.

When Wilhelm II became kaiser, Bismarck was removed from his position as chancellor because Wilhelm wanted more power. People in neighboring countries were concerned because they believed Germany had too much power already. During this period, countries in Europe frequently made and broke treaties and alliances in an attempt to prevent one country from becoming too powerful.

On June 28, 1914, Archduke Franz Ferdinand, the heir to the Austrian throne, and his wife were assassinated while they were in Bosnia Herzegovina. Due to the various alliances of countries in Europe at the time, this event led to World War I.

World War I lasted for four years, and when it was over, Germany had lost a large part of its population. Many cities were in ruins, and a great deal of the countryside had been destroyed. As a result of the Treaty of Versailles, a peace treaty signed in Versailles in 1919, Germany was forced to accept responsibility for the war and was required to pay large sums of money to countries it had opposed during the war. This led to a weak and poorly organized German government. Inflation was out of control; the cost of an item could increase between the morning and the afternoon. German currency had no real value, and the Germans suffered a severe depression.

Adolph Hitler and the Nazi party used the Germans' anger over the war debt and their desire to stop apologizing for the war to rise to power. Hitler held on to his power by jailing and executing people who disagreed with his policies. He believed in a master race of German people. He told the German people that the Jews were responsible for many of the hardships the Germans were experiencing. He instituted laws that prevented Jews, as well as others who did not fit within his master race, from owning property, working in certain jobs, and attending schools. Jews, Slavs, and even Gypsies, were rounded up and sent to concentration camps where they were forced to do hard labor and where millions were tortured and killed. The Germans began World War II under Hitler's leadership when they invaded Poland in September of 1939. Again, allies in Europe were forced to join together in a war to protect their borders and governments.

Two Germanys

World War II ended in 1945, and Germany was divided into four zones. One was controlled by the Soviet Union, and the other three by Great Britain, France, and the United States. Berlin was also divided into four zones. The Soviets wanted Germany to be a socialist state, but the British, French, and Americans wanted Germany to be a democracy.

During 1948 and 1949, the Soviets tried to seal Berlin off from the other German zones by closing all roads to Berlin from the western part of Germany. To prevent this, allied forces flew supplies into Berlin. This was called the Berlin Airlift. In 1949, Germany was divided into two countries, East Germany and West Germany, because no agreement could be reached on the way Germany should be governed.

In 1961, the Soviets and the East German government erected the Berlin Wall to prevent East Germans from having access to West Germany. The wall divided families and friends. It kept some people from being able to get to their jobs.

For forty-five years, the people of Germany were divided into the two countries of East Germany and West Germany. The governments of the two countries were very different. West Germans were allowed much more freedom politically, economically, and socially than the East German people. The East German government had to follow policies and laws dictated by the Soviet Union, many of which strictly limited personal movement and freedom.

German Reunification

In May 1989, Hungarians dismantled the barbed wire fences and guard posts that separated them from Austria. East Germans could go to Hungary and from there get to West Germany for the first time in many years. The East Germans were considered refugees and were entitled to West German citizenship and other benefits. More and more East Germans gathered in Hungary so they could go to West Germany. They were allowed to go into Austria and from there to West Germany. In time, other East Germans could get to West Germany by going to Czechoslovakia and taking special trains from there.

The Berlin Wall was destroyed on November 9, 1989. On October 3, 1990, the two Germanys were reunited into one with Helmut Kohl as chancellor. There will be many problems to solve as the two countries continue to merge. It will be a very expensive transformation. However, most Germans feel it will be worth the effort and expense to be able to enjoy a unified Germany once again.

In Your Classroom

Show the students maps of different periods in Germany's history from the times of Charlemagne, Bismarck, post-World War I and II, and after the German reunification. These maps may be found in books and encyclopedias.

Gather some newspaper and magazine articles and photographs of some of the events that led up to the reunification of Germany and the celebrations of reunification to share with students. Older students may help by visiting libraries or asking parents if they have any articles or photographs that they may have saved.

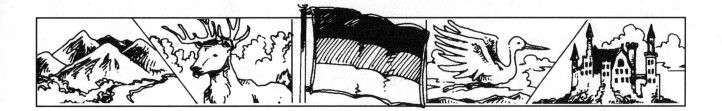

Language Expression

German, English, and Dutch are Germanic languages. There are many dialects spoken in the different regions of Germany. A person from the north of Germany might have difficulty communicating with a German from the south if each person speaks in his or her local dialect. All Germans learn to speak **High German**. It is the language taught in school, used in books and magazines, and spoken in films and on television.

Pronunciation

German is spoken crisply with each word pronounced clearly. Pronunciation rules are reasonably consistent:

Say **v** for **w**.
Say **i** as in b**i**te for **ei**.
Say **e** as in b**ea**t for **ie**.
Say **a** as in b**ai**t for **e**.
Say **oo** as in b**oo**t for **u**.
Say **k** for **ch**.
Say **a** as in f**a**ther for **a**.
Say **oy** as in b**oy** for **eu**.
Say **ou** as in r**ou**nd for **au**.

GUTEN TAG!

German Words and Phrases

Numbers from one to ten:

one	eins
two	zwei
three	drei
four	vier
five	fünf
six	sechs
seven	sieben
eight	acht
nine	neun
ten	zehn

Other vocabulary:

red	rot
green	grün
yellow	gelb
blue	blau
black	schwarz
white	weiss
book	das Buch
school	die Schule
children	die Kinder

Commonly-used expressions

I wish you a good appetite. ....Guten Appetit!
Good health ....Gesundheit
All is in order. ....Alles in Ordnung.
Good day ....Guten Tag
Goodbye.....................................Auf Wiedersehen
Thank you ....Danke
I am glad to see you. ....Ich freue mich, Sie zu sehen.

In Your Classroom

Place German books and pamphlets in the book area of your classroom. Try to find magazines and newspapers written in German. See the Additional Resources section for books written in English that are about Germany.

All nouns are capitalized when they are written in German. Write stories the German way by capitalizing all the nouns. Let the children illustrate the stories and share them with the class.

Label articles in the room with their German names, and use some German words in daily speech. Greet each other with Guten Tag (good day).

Learn to count in German, and practice simple math problems.

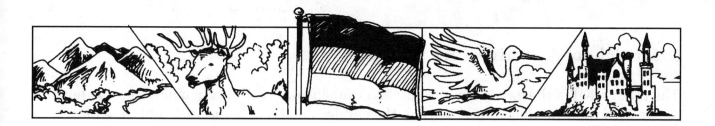

Daily Life

Money

The basic unit of currency is the **Deutsche Mark**. It is divided into 100 Pfennigs.

Clothing

In southern Germany, many people still wear traditional clothing. Men often wear **Lederhosen**, short-trousered overalls made out of leather, and **alpine hats**, and women wear **Dirndls**, full-skirted dresses with fitted bodices. Most Germans wear clothes that are very similar to those worn in America.

School

School begins at 8:00 a.m. and ends by 12:30 or 1:00 p.m. School is in session six days a week, Monday through Saturday. Children may go to kindergarten when they are three years old. All children must begin **Grundschule**, basic school, when they are six years old.

After four to six years of schooling, children and their parents decide which kind of secondary school they will attend. A **Hauptschule** is a secondary school that offers some job training. A **Realschule** is a vocational school. Classes at a **Gymnasium** prepare students to go on to a university.

Classrooms in Germany are more formal than American classrooms. German students are very courteous to their teachers. When a teacher enters a classroom, students stand and greet him or her. Students usually say, **"Guten Morgen, Herr Lehrer (or Frau Lehrerin)."** ("Good morning, teacher.") Older students are often called by their last names instead of their first names.

All students study some of the same subjects no matter which kind of school they attend. They have classes in German language, literature, a foreign language, history, art, music, math, and science. Germans value education and learning throughout their lives. There are also many adult education classes in Germany which teach about specific jobs as well as many other subjects that people are interested in learning.

After School Activities and Sports

The main meal of the day is usually served at lunchtime, so German children come home to eat with their families. After eating, the children do their homework and then play with friends or watch television.

German children like to go to sports clubs to play after school and on weekends. At the clubs, they swim and play soccer, handball, table tennis, and other games. During their free time, many German families enjoy walking and riding bikes. Many people enjoy skiing in the winter.

German schools do not have sports programs. People who want to play a sport join an organization. The soccer organization is very popular. It has over four million members including children, teenagers, adults, and professional players. Many people are soccer fans and go to the games played by professional teams.

Housing

The majority of Germans live in apartments, though many people have houses. Most German families have fewer than three children. As a result, apartments and houses are built for small families. Rooms are small, and the furniture is small or built into the apartment walls. Many German children have their own rooms, but children of the same sex may share a bedroom. People sleep under **duvets** (comforters made of feathers and down) called feather beds. On sunny days, the duvets are hung over window sills so they can freshen in the air. Because yards are small or not available, most German children belong to athletic clubs.

Though most Germans live in cities, many still love to garden. Many German homes and apartments are decorated by window boxes. Some Germans who live in apartments buy or lease small gardens near their cities. They work in these gardens during their leisure time and grow flowers and vegetables. Some of the gardens have enough space for a small house so the owners may stay for a weekend.

In Your Classroom

Make window boxes to decorate the windows of the classroom. Use half-gallon milk cartons to make the window boxes. Cut out one side, rinse well, fill with soil, and add flower seeds. Let children examine seeds to see that each type of flower has a different kind of seed. Children may make charts to see which seeds sprout first and grow fastest. Keep some gardening books in the classroom.

German Manners

Manners in Germany tend to be more formal than in the United States, although younger people are less formal than their elders. Shopkeepers are always greeted when people enter the stores, and they are thanked when people leave. People in Germany usually shake hands to greet friends when they meet on the street or in each other's homes.

In Your Classroom

Help children organize the information they have been learning about Germany by making a mural of a typical German day. Have children make a list of things they want to include in the mural. Let children refer to the books about Germany in your book area for ideas of what to include. Objects for the mural may be drawn, painted, cut-out, and glued together. Be imaginative!

Shake each child's hand, and encourage children to shake the hands of classmates when they arrive at school in the morning. Have children greet teachers and the principal when they enter the classroom in the typical way that German students do—by standing and saying, **"Guten Tag, Herr _____ or Frau _____ ."** ("Good day, Mr. _____ or Mrs. _____ .")

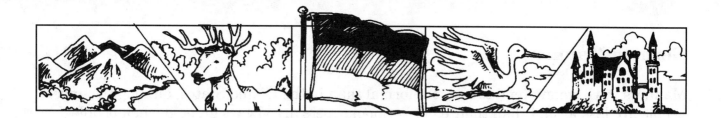

Foods

In Germany people usually eat breakfast early in the morning. Breakfast usually consists of rolls, cheese, cold-cuts, and jam and butter. In the mid-morning, Germans eat a "second breakfast" of a small sandwich. The main meal is usually eaten at mid-day. The evening meal is often sandwiches or sausages eaten with cheese and salad. People in Germany like to go to coffee houses in the afternoon. They buy something to drink and a piece of **Torte** or **Kuchen** (cake) to eat.

Recipes

Apple strudel is a popular dessert in Germany. It is served warm with whipped cream. The pastry in the strudel is made by stretching the dough until it is paper thin. The recipe below uses phyllo dough instead of making the pastry from scratch.

Apple Strudel

4 medium apples peeled and sliced very thin
1/8 cup raisins
1/4 cup sugar
1/4 cup blanched almonds
1/2 teaspoon ground cinnamon
1/4 teaspoon ground cloves
6 sheets of thawed phyllo pastry
1 stick of butter, melted
1/4 cup fine dry breadcrumbs

Combine the first six ingredients. Place one sheet of phyllo on a damp towel, lightly brush with butter. Layer five more sheets of phyllo, one at a time, brushing each with butter. Sprinkle bread crumbs on the top layer. Spread apple mixture over phyllo leaving a two inch border all around. Fold all edges over two inches. Starting at the end of one of the long sides, roll, using jelly roll method. Place seam side down on a lightly greased cookie sheet. Brush with butter. Bake at 375 degrees for 30 minutes. Cool on wire racks. Slice and serve with whipped cream.

Hot Potato Salad

6 freshly boiled potatoes, sliced
4 strips of bacon, crumbled
1 dill pickle, chopped
1 small onion, chopped
3 celery stalks, chopped
1/4 cup of water
1/2 cup of vinegar
1/2 teaspoon sugar
1/2 teaspoon salt
1/4 teaspoon paprika

Saute onion and celery until golden. Heat the last five ingredients to boiling. Mix all the ingredients together, and serve hot. This salad is also good to eat when it is cold.

Potato Pancakes

4 large potatoes, peeled and grated into shreds (or 2 1/2 cups when shredded)
1 onion, grated
2 tablespoons flour
2 large eggs
1/8 teaspoon pepper
1/8 teaspoon salt
vegetable oil

Mix the grated potatoes, the grated onion, and the flour together in a large bowl. In a smaller bowl, combine the eggs with the salt and pepper and beat with a fork. Then add the egg mixture to the potato mixture, and mix all together.

To fry the pancakes, pour a bit of oil in the bottom of a skillet and heat over medium to medium-high heat. Put a tablespoonful of the potato mixture into the skillet, and flatten into pancake shape with the spoon. When the edges brown, turn pancake over and cook the other side until its edges brown. Remove pancake from skillet and drain in paper towels. Continue this frying process until all the potato mixture has been used. You can cook several pancakes in the skillet at the same time. For a sweet and tasty treat, eat with applesauce, or for a hearty meal, serve the pancakes with cooked sausage.

Sandwiches

German sandwiches are usually served open-faced and are eaten with a knife and fork. Make German style sandwiches using dark rye bread or a dense wheat bread. Butter the bread, and spread a German style mustard on each slice. Add corned beef or ham and Swiss or Gouda cheese.

Marzipan

Germans enjoy **marzipan**, a colorful and artistically crafted candy. Most candy stores and coffee houses have beautiful marzipan candies for sale. Marzipan is often shaped and colored to look like fruit or animals. At holiday times, marzipan is made with holiday themes.

Marzipan can be purchased in rolls. Its texture is similar to bread dough. Let children enjoy shaping marzipan into fruits or animals. They can then paint their candy creations with diluted vegetable coloring.

In Your Classroom

Prepare and serve a typical evening meal (more like our lunch) for the children's lunch. Children may make the German-style sandwiches. Apples, pears, and grapes may be washed and placed in bowls. Apple strudel or marzipan could be made for dessert. Children may try eating European style, keeping the fork in the left hand and the knife in the right hand.

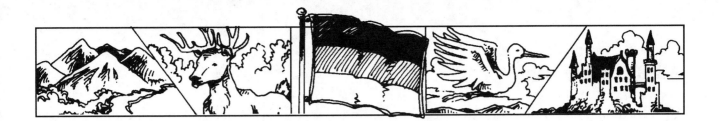

Games

Children play many games with their friends during school recess or at each others' homes. Some of the games they play are very similar to games played by children in the United States. Below are some games that German children play and that you can play in your classrooms.

One, Two, Three, Who Has the Ball?

Children stand in a row with their hands behind their backs. One child is "It." "It" stands several feet away from the other children with his or her back to them. One of the children in the row holds a small ball in his or her hand. The children chant "ONE, TWO, THREE, WHO HAS THE BALL?" "It" walks towards the child that he or she thinks has the ball. If "It" is correct, then he or she is "It" again. If "It" is incorrect, the child with the ball runs to a base. "It" must tag the child before he or she reaches the base to remain "It." If the child with the ball reaches the base before being tagged, then he or she becomes "It." The objective is to remain "It."

Change, Change Little Tree

This game is typically played in a wooded area in Germany. If there are no trees around, circles may be drawn on the ground to represent trees or other objects may be used as bases. Each child stands beside a tree, or a base called a tree. The child who is "It" stands in the middle of all the children and calls "CHANGE, CHANGE LITTLE TREE." All the children must run to a new tree, or base, while "It" tries to tag a child. The child who is tagged becomes the new "It." If "It" does not tag anybody, then that child remains "It" until he or she tags somebody.

All Birds Fly High

Children sit in a circle and clap their hands on their knees. One child or the teacher acts as the leader and says "ALL BIRDS LIFT HANDS." The children lift their hands and then resume clapping. The leader then says "ALL MOSQUITOES LIFT HANDS." The children lift their hands and then resume clapping. The leader may then say "ALL TABLESPOONS LIFT HANDS." The children should continue clapping, but should not lift their hands after the leader's phrase. Each time the leader's phrase includes an animal or object that flies (kites, bees, butterflies, helicopters, and so on), the children lift their hands and then resume clapping. If the phrase does not include an animal or object that flies (dogs, pencils, children, and so on), the children should keep clapping and not lift their hands. Other categories (farm animals, colors, nouns, verbs, number pairs that equal ten, and words beginning with various letters of the alphabet) may be used with this game to reinforce concepts being learned by the students.

Little Bird Say Peep

Children sit on chairs in a circle. The child who is "It" stands in the middle of the circle and is blindfolded. All the children quietly change chairs. The teacher takes "It" to a child in the circle, and the two children hold hands. All the children chant "LITTLE BIRD SAY PEEP." The child holding "Its" hand says "PEEP." "It" tries to guess who the child is. If "It" guesses the child's name correctly, he or she remains "It." If "It" guesses incorrectly, the child holding "Its" hand becomes the new "It."

In Your Classroom

Play some of the games listed above with the students during a recreational time.

Arts and Sciences

Fairy Tales

Germany is famous for its fairy tales collected by the Grimm brothers. Fairy tales are a part of Germany's cultural heritage, and they are loved by children all over the world.

In Your Classroom

Share some of the famous Grimm fairy tales with your students. Have students write their own fairy tales and share them with the rest of the class. Younger children may dictate their stories to the teacher and draw pictures to accompany them. Make a mural out of construction paper illustrating various favorite fairy tale characters.

Read the book *The Jolly Postman* by Janet and Allan Ahlberg. (See the Additional Resources section.) This book includes letters written to fairy tale characters from other fairy tale characters. Children may then write their own letters to one of their favorite fairy tale characters. Older children may want to write as though they were fairy tale characters themselves.

Puppets

Many wooden toys and puppets are made and enjoyed in Germany. Marionettes are puppets moved by strings attached to the puppet from a T-bar handle. Life-like movements are created by tilting the T-bar and by lifting individual strings. Marionette shows were a popular form of entertainment in Germany's royal courts and remain popular with Germans today.

In Your Classroom

Some of the fairy tales especially enjoyed by the class may be re-enacted by making simple marionettes and finger and hand puppets to represent fairy tale characters. Divide children into small groups to create puppet shows of these fairy tales.

Music

Germany has a rich musical history. Much of the classical music we enjoy and study today was composed by German musicians. These musicians include Johann Sebastian Bach, George Frideric Handel, Ludwig Van Beethoven, and Richard Wagner.

Folk songs also hold a very important place in German culture. Many are very well known and are often sung by people when they are celebrating and having fun.

In Your Classroom

Introduce children to some of Germany's famous composers by playing selections of their music for students. Include J.S. Bach's *Brandenburg Concertos*, Handel's *Water Music*, and Beethoven's *Eroica*. Tell children the story of *Die Meistersinger von Nürnberg* (*The Mastersingers of Nuremberg*) by Wagner, and play the *Heavenly Morning* aria. Introduce the *Hansel and Gretel* opera by Engleburt Humperdinck by reading *Behind the Golden Curtain* by E. Lee Spruyt. This book tells about the behind-the-scenes preparations needed to produce *Hansel and Gretel* at the Metropolitan Opera House. Then show students the video cassette of this opera as performed by the Metropolitan Opera.

Artists

Three of Germany's greatest artists were Albrecht Dürer, Hans Holbein the Younger, and Paul Klee. Dürer and Holbein were contemporaries in the sixteenth century. Klee was an artist of the early twentieth century.

Albrecht Dürer was a painter and printmaker best known for the woodcuts and engravings he created to make his prints. His woodcuts were more detailed and graceful than others created at that time.

Hans Holbein the Younger painted portraits of many of the famous people of his time.

Paul Klee was influenced by primitive art, the drawings of young children, and Cubism, a style using geometric forms—primarily cubes.

In Your Classroom

Use prints, posters, and postcards to introduce children to the works of these artists. Some libraries may have prints or posters that can be borrowed. Museum shops will carry postcards of the works of various artists. Encourage students to discuss similarities and differences in the works of the three artists.

Let students experience printmaking as exemplified by Dürer by making sponge or potato prints. Younger children will need pre-cut sponges or potatoes; older children may be able to make their own. After the sponges or potatoes are ready, dip them in paint and press them onto paper.

After sharing some of the portraits painted by Holbein, pair up your students, and have them take turns drawing portraits of each other. Remind them to start by drawing a head and then adding hair, eyebrows, eyes, ears, a nose, and a mouth.

Klee used many geometric forms in his work. Have children use paints and markers to create their own pictures out of geometric forms.

Germany has many lovely museums. After the children have finished their pictures, set up a museum in a corner of the classroom. Use the children's pictures and the artists' prints and postcards to nurture an appreciation for artistic interpretations and abilities.

Inventors, Inventions, and Scientists

Over 400 years ago, Johannes Gutenberg invented a printing press with moveable type. The Chinese had long ago invented printing with moveable type, but because the Chinese language was so complex and involved so many individual characters, the printing method did not develop there. Printing, as we know it today, was invented by Gutenberg. Because of his invention, books no longer had to be copied by hand. They became more readily available and allowed more people to share ideas.

Gabriel Fahrenheit invented a system of measuring heat and cold. Fahrenheit degrees have been used since the 1700s.

Gottlieb Daimler, Karl Benz, Rudolf Diesel, and Felix Wankel were inventors of the internal combustion engines which led to the cars and trucks we have today.

Bicycles, x-ray machines, electric trains, and pocket watches were all invented by Germans.

Albert Einstein was a physicist who won a Nobel prize for his discoveries. He left Germany to come to the United States to escape the Nazis.

Wernher Von Braun also left Germany to escape the Nazis. He was a rocket engineer and was involved in the development of the U.S. space program.

In Your Classroom

Take children to visit a printing press at a print shop or newspaper publishing company.

Set up a print shop in your classroom with rubber stamps and ink pads. Children may use these to create their own books, cards, and posters.

Use a thermometer with Fahrenheit degrees to measure the temperature outdoors everyday at the same time. Make a graph of the temperatures.

Display some pictures of early automobiles, bicycles, x-ray machines, and pocket watches. Discuss the idea of inventions. They are ideas people come up with to fill a need or a desire for something. Have the students list ideas for inventions of things they might need or enjoy having. Give them a chance to be inventors by having them draw their inventions and/or write (or tell) about them. Older children might be able to actually create simple inventions. Display the children's work in the classroom or school library.

Display photographs showing the progression from early rockets to the shuttles used by the space program today. Add some books to the class library about rockets and space. Make a model of a rocket as a class project. Make a mural of the solar system. Have each child make a page of a book for the class about a question they have about rockets or space, or make a book about what each child would like to visit in space.

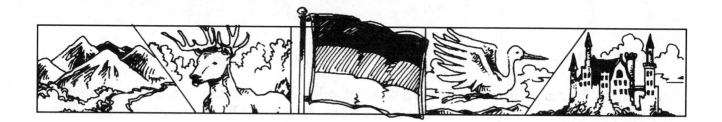

Holidays

Fasching or Karneval

Fasching is a pre-Lenten celebration, similar to Mardi Gras in New Orleans. It is also a festival which welcomes spring and celebrates the end of winter. In some areas of Germany, people, especially children, dress in costumes just as children in the United States do for Halloween. They participate in parades and have parties at school. In the Black Forest, people dress in costumes and wooden masks. They frighten winter spirits away with loud noises.

In Your Classroom

Children may make masks using large paper bags, pre-cut heavy paper, or poster board. Let them decorate masks with feathers, buttons, sequins, yarn, and markers.

Easter

At Easter time, German people decorate eggs by painting them with geometric or floral designs or pictures. Some eggs are dyed, and the dye is scraped away to form the design. Usually the eggs are pierced at each end and the contents are blown out. Other eggs are left intact. The contents dry up after several months. After the eggs have been decorated, they are hung on an egg tree. The tree is made by putting flowering branches in a vase.

The Easter rabbit hides eggs for children to find on Easter morning. The eggs are usually hidden outside. Children in different parts of Germany prepare for the visit from the Easter rabbit in various ways. Some children make rabbit gardens using grasses and decorations, others make moss nests, and some children have baskets in which to place the eggs they find. Later in the day, children play games with their eggs. They may roll them, have relay races, or have egg eating contests.

In Your Classroom

Younger children may decorate wooden or hardboiled eggs with markers. Older children may use paint and small paintbrushes to decorate the eggs. Allow children to display their eggs in a basket, moss nest, or rabbit garden.

St. Martin's Day

On November 11, children celebrate St. Martin's Day. Children make paper lanterns which they carry in a procession led by St. Martin on horseback. St. Martin pantomimes tearing his cloak to share it with a beggar. There are fireworks after the procession, and children receive candy and fruit in small sacks. At some schools, a campfire is built. Children sing and listen to the story of St. Martin sharing his cloak with a beggar. Then they share a large loaf of bread shaped like the saint.

In Your Classroom

Students may make paper lanterns out of lunch sacks. They may cut designs out of the sacks, and then color them. Attach each decorated sack to a stick with a short piece of string. Children may have their own procession on the playground.

Have students use bread dough to form a large St. Martin to bake and share, or have them bake individual St. Martin shaped breads that they may take home.

St. Nicholas Day

Another special holiday for children is St. Nicholas Day. On December 5, St. Nicholas and his servant Ruprecht visit German children. St. Nicholas looks like a Catholic bishop and was the historical figure from whom Santa Claus was modeled. Ruprecht is dressed in a hooded dark robe, and his face is covered. St. Nicholas and Ruprecht bring gifts in person to some children. Other children leave their shoes outside their front doors or on a window sill on the evening before St. Nicholas Day. Ruprecht leaves sticks and coal in naughty children's shoes. Good children receive small toys, candies, and a bundle of gilt sticks to remind them to be good. Many stores in Germany sell Ruprecht dolls made out of prunes and toothpicks.

In Your Classroom

Try making a Ruprecht doll in your classroom. Place two prunes lengthwise on a toothpick to create a body. An additional prune may be speared on a separate toothpick and placed on the body to create a head. Arms and legs may be formed by spearing prunes with toothpicks and placing them on the body. Raisins or other bits of dried fruit may be used for facial features, hands, and feet.

Christmas

The Christmas season starts in Germany in November. Many cities and towns have special Christmas markets that sell decorations, gifts, and holiday foods. These are called **Christkindlesmarkts**. The largest Christkindlesmarkt is in Nuremberg.

Christmas trees are an important part of the Christmas celebrations. A German legend tells of Martin Luther decorating a small fir tree with candles on Christmas eve to show his family how beautiful the woods were at night. Many German families decorate their trees on Christmas eve instead of earlier in the Christmas season. Handmade ornaments, small gifts, cookies, and candies decorate many German Christmas trees as well as candles or electric lights.

On Christmas Eve, many families open gifts, attend Midnight Mass, and come home to a festive supper. Christmas itself is a quiet day spent with the family. The day after Christmas is a holiday traditionally spent visiting friends.

In Your Classroom

Children may make ornaments from self-hardening clay. The ornaments can be painted or colored with markers when they have dried.

Create a market in your classroom using tables and desks as stalls. Children may take turns buying items from and selling items to each other. Items may include fruits, cookies, juice, and small ornaments or toys.

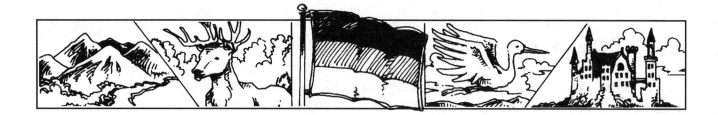

Additional Resources

Resources for Teachers and Children

Adler, Ann. *Passport to West Germany*. New York: Franklin Watts Inc., 1986.

Adler, Ann. *A Family in West Germany*. Minneapolis: Lerner Publications, 1985.

Ahlberg, Janet, and Allan Ahlberg. *The Jolly Postman or Other People's Letters*. Boston: Little, Brown and Company, 1986. A story of a postman's visit to several fairy tale characters. It includes the letters they receive.

Bradley, John, and Catherine Bradley. *Germany: The Reunification of a Nation*. New York: Aladdin Books, 1991.

Dornberg, John. *The Two Germanys*. New York: Dial Books, 1974.

Einhorn, Barbara. *West Germany*. New York: The Bookwright Press, 1988.

Hintz, Martin. *Enchantment of the World: West Germany*. Chicago: Children's Press, 1983.

James, Ian. *Inside West Germany*. New York: Franklin Watts, 1988.

Janson, H. W., and Anthony Janson, eds. *History of Art for Young People*. New York: Harry N. Abrams, 1987.

Kirby, George. *Looking at Germany*. Lippincott Jr. Books, 1972.

The Late Middle Ages. History of the World. Milwaukee: Raintree Publishers Limited Partnership, 1990.

Macaulay, David. *Castle*. New York: The Trumpet Club, 1977.

MacDonald, Fiona. *A Medieval Castle*. New York: Peter Bedrick Books, 1990.

McKenna, David. *Places and Peoples of the World: East Germany*. New York: Chelsea House Publishers, 1988.

Parnell, Helga. *Cooking the German Way*. Minneapolis: Lerner Publications, 1987.

Pfeiffer, Christine. *Germany, Two Nations, One Heritage*. Minneapolis: Dillon Press, Inc., 1987.

Pitcher, Caroline. *Build Your Own Castle*. New York: Aladdin Books Ltd., 1985.

Rosenberg, Jane. *Sing Me a Story*. London: Thames and Hudson, 1989. The stories of several operas are told and illustrated.

Seger, Gerhart H. *Germany*. The Fideler Company, 1978.

Sharman, Tim. *We Live in East Germany*. New York: Franklin Watts, 1984.

Spruyt, E. Lee. *Behind the Golden Curtain, Hansel and Gretel at the Great Opera House*. New York: Four Winds Press, 1986.

Stadtler, Christa. *We Live in West Germany*. New York: Franklin Watts, 1984.

Ventura, Piero. *Great Composers*. New York: G. P. Putnam's Sons, 1988.

Ventura, Piero. *Great Painters*. New York: G. P. Putnam's Sons, 1984.

Wright, David K., Rhoda Irene Sherwood, and Scott Enk, eds. *Children of the World: West Germany*. Milwaukee: Gareth Stevens, Inc., 1988.

Wright, Lyndie. *Puppets*. New York: Franklin Watts, 1989. Gives easy to follow directions to make a variety of puppets.

General Resources

Bettelheim, Bruno. *The Uses of Enchantment, The Meaning and Importance of Fairy Tales*. New York: Alfred A. Knopf, 1976. Gives the reasons fairy tales are so important to children as well as recommendations for telling the stories.

Embassy of the Federal Republic of Germany, 4645 Reservoir Road NW, Washington, DC 20007.

German National Tourist Board, 747B Third Ave., 33rd Floor, New York, NY 10017 or 444 S. Flower St., Suite 2230, Los Angeles, CA 90071.

Opie, Iona, and Peter Opie. *The Classic Fairy Tales*. New York: Oxford University Press, 1974. Gives a historical perspective of several popular fairy tales and changes that have occurred to the stories over the years.

Fairy Tales

(Books are listed by illustrator. All tales are stories collected by the Grimm brothers.)

Adams, Adrienne. *Hansel and Gretel*. New York: Charles Scribner's Sons, 1975.

Adams, Adrienne. *Jorinda and Joringel*. New York: Charles Scribner's Sons, 1968.

Brett, Jan. *Goldilocks and the Three Bears*. New York: Sandcastle, 1987.

Burkert, Nancy Ekholm. *Snow White and the Seven Dwarfs*. Translated by Randall Jarrell. New York: Farrar, Straus, and Giroux, 1972.

Gag, Wanda. *Tales From Grimm*. New York: Coward-McCann, Inc., 1936.

Gag, Wanda. *More Tales from Grimm*. New York: Coward-McCann, Inc., 1947.

Hoffmann, Felix. *Rapunzel*. New York: Harcourt, Brace and Company, 1960.

Mayer, Mercer. *The Sleeping Beauty*. New York: Macmillan Publishing Company, 1984.

Plume, Ilse. *The Bremen Town Musicians*. New York: Doubleday and Company, Inc., 1980.

Ormerod, Jan. *The Frog Prince*. New York: Lothrop, 1990.

Sanderson, Ruth. *The Twelve Dancing Princesses*. Boston: Little, Brown and Company, 1990.

Sendak, Maurice. *Dear Mili*. New York: Farrar, Straus and Giroux, 1988.

Zelinsky, Paul O. *Rumpelstiltskin*. New York: E.P. Dutton, 1986.

Zwerger, Lisbeth. *The Seven Ravens*. New York: William Morrow and Company, 1981.